NHS
Forth Valley

Fighting For Every
Heartbeat
James McDonald

A donation from the sale of each book will go to
Forth Valley Royal Hospital's Cardiology department.

Dedication

To all my Family, friends and colleagues, on the other side, who touched my life on this. Amongst the many;

Mither & the McKenna Clan.
Faither & the McDonald Clan.
Barbara Hammond & the writers who performed lyrical gymnastics with the pen. Jim Campbell and the Scholars of the Bard.
Bobby Underhill & the brothers of the brush.

Mo Gille agus Nighean Breagha
Scott agus Joanne
R.I.P.

About the Author

James McDonald is a time served Painter & Decorator, recently retired after 48 years in the trade. Many of the poems in this collection were inspired by contracts he worked on (The Laird of Ben Alder, Sailing from Shawbost.) Incidents near some of his many work sites, (Swing for Her, The Waverley Beggar.) experiences with people he met (The Prisoner, The Wellman Clinic.) during that long career. As a lover of Burns and a speaker at numerous suppers he wrote and performed many of his own works, (Tam McAirthur's Drive, Walpurgis Nicht, Lindy Lou.)

His many other Interests also shaped his writing. A love of hill walking (Hard Wrocht) and over 25 years membership of his local Falkirk Writers' Circle (The Defiant Writer, The Tutor) which he combined very successfully during the years 1999-2000 to write Scotland on Sunday's Walk of The Day column following up with the Walk of the Week book, first published by Mercat Press in 2004, He now writes a column in the Writers Umbrella, a bi-monthly online magazine, which offers advice and encouragement to writers, wherever they are on their writing journey.

James has a long history of public voluntary service, taking groups hillwalking to raise money for charities. Bringing the Burns message into local hospitals and Old Folks Homes and for over twenty years he has been a member of Falkirk & District Arts and Civic Council, a public conduit organisation channelling the concerns of local groups to the appropriate persons or departments in the local Falkirk Council, as well as being organisers of the local Tryst Festival. He was honoured to be the organisations Chairman from 2008, when the town hosted the National Mhod, the annual celebration of Gaelic Music and Culture in Scotland, until 2010, which was, The Diamond Anniversary of Falkirk & District Arts and Civic Council. But his first love has always been; Writing, Performing and "Listening to Poetry."

Introduction

When Writers' reach a certain age, especially those who have been members of Writers' circle's or other writing groups for years, if not decades, they find themselves with volumes of work hidden away in files, drawers, or old briefcases. In the bottom of cupboards, in lofts, garden sheds or garages. Often forgotten about, but occasionally dusted down, tweaked then entered for another competition. If successful, it will be read out at the next group meeting or summer social. Maybe posted off to a specialist magazine, while the writer basks in a rosy glow of magnificence. After the handshakes and pats on the back the work is soon forgotten about without another thought of publication.

The writers' reasoning? The author needs to keep control of these; stories, articles or poems. And they are not going to be released to the wider world "till efter am deid!"

If I have a mission in the remaining fragile years of my existence, it will be to encourage these authors along with their undiscovered, bottom, middle and top drawer works to get into the public domain, so they can grab their share of the limelight, public acclimation and the fifteen minutes of fame they so richly deserve. Before they're Deid!

Contents

Listening to poetry

Nae loupin ower chairs or throwin o' dirks
Nae shepherdin sheep or herdin o' stirks
Nae kecklin oot loud or shuffling yer clugs
When listenin tae poesy Cock up yer lugs

Nae rustling o' papers or peppery pokes
Nae hoastin, or coughin, or clearin yer throats
Nae scratchin yer stibble, or onythin werse
Nor slurpin yer drinks when listening tae verse

Nae hee-haw or see-saw or marjory daw
Nae kissin the lassies nae maiter how braw
Nae slap and tickle or cuddlin yer Quine
And nae houghmagandie when listenin tae rhyme.

Jawin or crawin or speirin yer mate
Isnae allowed when the nichts drawin late
Jist listen intently tae whits bein said.
And gie the best order when poetry's read.

The Defiant Writer

The Denby cup was empty
Nae money oan the board
The committee member yelled wae rage
"Is it me yer trying tae goad?"
The chairman answered tearfully
Don't put the blame oan me
Its thon Defiant writer
That's no peyed for his tea.

The committee and the chairman
Looked panic stricken round
They searched the lounge bar high and low
But no writer could be found
We'll search again the toilet
It's the only place he'll be
'Cos wae drinking a' that Earl Grey
He'll hae hopped in for a pee.

The Defiant Writer

They rushed intae the toilet
Wae anger in their eyes,
The chairman roared triumphantly,
I think we've won a prize!
They found the writer huddled there
A notepad oan his knee
Wae eldritch shrieks they cried at him
"Ye've no peyed for yer tea!"

The committee member held his airms
The chairman grabbed his hair
A dipstick doon his throat they put
Twas mair than he could bear
The chairman pulled the dipstick oot
"There's evidence you see!"
A drop o' dark broon liquid
Twa inches o' cauld tea.

The Defiant Writer

They propped the martyred writer up
Darjeelin dreeped doon his jaw
They shot him wae a fountain pen
Against the midden wa'
Wae these immortal words he fell
Right doon oan wan patched knee
"For their country men have fought and died
But I'm dying for my tea!"

Cairney At Fawkirk

Ower the week ye laid bare your life
Fower lives? Or wis it mair?
Oan yer stravaigins tae New Zealand.
Bit aye ye come back tae Scotland. Yer tap root.

And as ye turned that tap
Oot poured McGonnigal and Service
Stevenson and Burns
Walkin aside ye like leerie men
Lichtin the streets o' Fawkirk.

The Bairns? Nivver twitched their nets!

But your men o' genius are a' river fowk
The Tay, the Doon, the Forth and Clyde.
Fawkirk's hemmed in wae canals.

But them that came
Saw these great rivers
Flow aside ye
As yer licht burned aff the haar.

The Fawkirk Corbie

In thon kirkyard thir lies a knight
And tho' his baines hiv lang turned white
Folk come tae worship his sword and mace
And scatter grub a' ower the place.

The toon gulls hiv' a nest ower there
And they've been frisky, a second year pair.
If I leave them jist a month tae thrive
Some coddled eggs will be my prize.

And as I go searchin in the early light. The
Young squabs are stampin the grund for a bite.
Their dancing feet bring the early worm,
When I scare them off twill be my turn.

The Laird of Ben Alder

Oh Laird of Ben Alder
As it gets caulder
Ye eywis jet aff
Tae sunnier climes
Wae the grouse shootin done
And the stag trophies won
Ye pack up yer Purdies
And go aff quaffin steins.

In pounds yer worth millions
In French francs its billions
In Lire? They aint found a name for it yet
And the promissory note
For the hoose that ye bought
Wad pey aff half o' the national debt.

The Laird of Ben Alder

Ye spent a' yer riches
Oan gold plated switches
Ye spent massive sums
Oan auld fashioned lums
Oan a machine tae starch collars
Ye spent fists fu' o' dollars
And ye built a gymnasium
For shrinkin yer tums

But ye brought work tae the Errit
And that's tae yer credit
Tho' half o' that work force
Wis foreign, aye that's true
Wae a wee bit o' thocht
A' that workforce ye brocht
Could a' been supplied
By oor ain local broo.

The Laird of Ben Alder

Fae the Auld Spanish Main
Ye brocht a man wae a chain
Tae make a' yer new wid
Wizened and aged
Tae make yer wid aulder
There's Big Finlay Calder
Wad hit it wae Tackity Buits
And wee stanes.

A' the wey up frae Lundin
Ye brocht Maxi Mullion
Tae hing up yer curtains
Oan windaes and wa's
If ye dangled a carrot
Wee Teen fae the garret
Wad hing a' the
Swags and Tails for yer balls.

The Laird of Ben Alder

Tae look efter yer cellar
Ther wis thon wee French fellar
He boaked in a pail
Every drink that he taen
Well he might no hae manners
And wae ten drinks he stammers
But the best man for vino
Is Red Biddy McBayne.

It's a year noo precisely
And ye've settled quite nicely
Tho' the Lodge o' Ben Alder
Will ne'er be the same
We built ye a hoose
Wae yer chainge that wis loose
We built ye a hoose
Noo mak' it a hame.

Hard Wrocht

"Hard Gawn! Naethin bit Heather and hard places!"
Shouts the backpacker ladent doon wae Munro's.
But only a walker wi' Sir Hugh o' Lindertis in his bag
Wad shout "Naethin but heather!"
Tae a rambler, seein not only the heather, but
Rowan berries hingin' frae a stunted tree
Growin frae the threshold o' a lang neglecktit biggan.
A biggan cleared tae mak wey for sheep.

Whaur noo, Descendants o' thir black faced sheep,
Skip ower rubble, streechin legs and necks, tae reach the
tender leaves o' blaeberry
Sproutin fae gable wa's.
Aye, nuthin but hard places tae tickers o' lists.
But traipsers tae the hills will recognise;
Derelict crofts whaur the kail crops turned wild
Lang Time Syne.

Hard Wrocht

And among the hard places, they'll see
Hearth stanes and lintels, whaur thistle down
Hame in oan feathery parachutes.

And they'll ken anither place, a place whaur
Wild primrose button the hillside, a place whaur
Harebells nod tae common butterflies
Blue as the winter chills
And they'll know where seven war spent men
Dug their drains and staked their claims, oan
Brockets land, for the right tae feed their weans.

Hard gawn? Nuthin bit heather and hard places?
Aye! Tae tickers o' lists.

Recession

The sun rises
But finds it hard
To breach the trees branches
Where the broad leaves
Shade the forest floor

A forest floor
Carpeted with fallen leaves
That choke the life
From lesser plants and trees

'Til wrapped
In its own decay
The forest fades away.

The Sculpture

A shapeless feature from the rear
Then as it turns
Its form becomes clear
A moment of passion
Frozen in stone
No flesh nor hair
No skeletal bone

But the lovers kiss
And the warmth is there
With the sculptors
Art, that we now share.

The Waverley Beggar

I'm hameless and hungry
Have ye any loose chainge
Asks the beggar oan the Waverley steps
Cross legged, he sits
Wae his hat oan the grund
Collecting pennies as they roll doon the wynd,

You know it used to be buskers
And ye went passing bye
The conscience wisnae quite pricked the same
It was street entertainment
It was culture, if you like
And for the busker?
The slim chance of fame.

But how dae ye pass a beggar
Oan the steps, that's hungry
and no got a hame.

Lindy Lou

When Dead eye Dick met Lindy Lou
A girl from the upper strand
Dead eye made designs on Lou
Now don't misunderstand
Dead eye was no Picasso
Or artist in tattoo
No Dead eye Dick had devised a plan
To get the kit off Lindy Lou.

He asked her to a picture show
Thinking that would be enough
He bought popcorn a diet coke
And a bag of candy puff
When the lights went down
Amidst the flickerin sound
The moment he saw fit
He gently snaked his arm around
And tried to slip the mitt.

Lindy Lou

But Lindy Lou was too cute for Dick
She had second guessed his plan
She wore three coats a pullover
And some underwear... Now banned
Although she was sweatin buckets
It was summertime you see
Dead eye Dick and his wily tricks
Couldnae lay a finger on Lou's knee.

But every girl has her price
And Dead eye knew the score
So he offered Lou a tenner
Prepared to pay out more
"I've never been with a feller
On a date or a one night stand,
But if you want to get my kit off
It'll cost you a cool grand."

Lindy Lou

Now Dead eye Dick was minted
But he tried to negotiate
Though charms you have a plenty
Your way above the going rate
The price I offer is fair and good
For a girl taking off her kit
But give a star performance
And there's an extra couple of quid.

Now Lindy's hopes of getting rich
Were dealt a cruel blow
And as for Dick's proposal
She would have to answer no
But she knew that Dick was loaded
So she gave it one last try
"Well, I'll let you see my womanhood
But only with one eye."

Lindy Lou

They struck the bargain there and then
With high fives and a spit
They sorted out a time and place
For Lou to strip her kit
A bargain one eyed view of Lou
Would be Dick's lustful prize
But he would have to pay a thousand pounds
If he opened up both eyes.

The place they chose was the Grand Hotel
A nice touch on Lindy's part
And on the night in question
She rolled up in her cart
Dick was already waiting
He had reserved the royal suite
To watch Lindy Lou's performance
He pulled up a bedside seat.

Lindy Lou

Before I start to strut my stuff
Some rules I'll have to ply
So you won't attempt to cheat me
You'll wear a black patch o'er one eye
And if you lift the black patch up
Or it falls down to the ground
A grand to me you'll pay this day
And then I'll leave the town.

She peeled her clothes off one by one
With the skill of a perfect tease
And as Dead eye Dick grew fidgety
She dropped her blouse onto his knees
He was thrilled tae bits when she bared her pits
But when he saw her furry mound
His eyes they popped the black patch flew off
And he lost a thousand pounds.

Lindy Lou

Lindy Lou left town that night
With a cool grand in her hand
And she headed east to Blackness Beach
To stretch out by the sand
But the quiet life was not for Lou
As her fame began to grow
So she high-tailed it to the Roxy
To join a burlesque show.

Now she tops the billing every night
With a twenty one man band
And she strips her mini-kilts off
To tunes from Jimmy Shand
And at ever star performance
Applauding each discarded strand
Sits Dead eye Dick the luckiest guy
To ever lose a thousand pounds.

Walpurgis Nicht

While driving along a tree lined road
I could feel in my bones,
there wis evil abroad
It was getting near midnight
The dark witchin' oor
When I saw a licht gleamin
But wisnae quite shure
So I got oot o' my car tae hae a guid look
Through the trees and the bushes
And the nicht, dark as soot.

I thocht I heard music frae just up the track,
And I spiered tae masel "Is it forward or back"
The music grew louder
"I could hear it quite clear!"
And it came frae a church
That's been shut forty year.

Walpurgis Nicht

That kirk wis taen ower by a devilish crowd,
Oan pews and the aisles they tumbled and roued
Wae wummin half drunk and barin' their all
I could see for masel, they were havin a ball
No a drink had I taen I was half weys insane
Tae see a' that drink and me getting nane.

I'd hae done sumthin aboot it
But by the powers I was sent
No the powers o' darkness
But the Lords gid intent.

I pushed back my shouthers
I held masel' straight
The deil and his crowd
Is sumthin I hate.

Walpurgis Nicht

I braced masel as I walked tae the door
Should I run back or go oan and explore
I wish I could say that the answer was mine
But my boady was taen ower by a celestial kind.

The doors they flew open, I wisnae masel
As I tackled the sons and dochters o' hell
They fell ever backwards, I came oan like a tide
I grew ever stronger wi' the lord oan my side
Auld Nick wis in front noo I widnae relent
Then a dunt tae my heid,
The powers? They were spent.

I came tae in a kirkyard
And I'll never be shaer
If the sichts I had seen
Had ever been there.

Tam McAirthur's Drive

When traffic wardens leave the street
And folk walk hame through rain and sleet
And corner grocers sit and wait
For wifies buyin their bread o'er late
While we sit in the Higginsneuk
Tryin tae squeeze a facial plook.
We think no oan the traffic cop
Wi' his Volvo car and licht oan top
Oor pie and beans getting burnt at hame
By the wummin ye married... Whit's her name
Standin wae her face in pleats
Plottin yer death whilst ironin' the sheets.

This truth found honest Tam McAirthur
As he drove hame ae nicht frae Airth sir
Auld Airth whaur every toon surpasses
Its better seen withoot yer glasses.

Ocht aye, but tae oor tale—One Friday nicht
Tam had got plastered, legless ticht.
At his elba, his baccy bag
Foo o' stoor that yince wis shag.
Tam wad smoke wan then sumday else's
He wad dae the same wae yer whisky glesses.

Tam McAirthur's Drive

But pleasures are like poppies spread,
Remembrance day... The memory's dead.
Or better still like snaw aff a dyke
Ye've had yer fun noo oan yer bike.
Nae man can tether time nor tide
At drinkin up time Tams outside.

In his Fiat Panda wae three push starts
A cloud o' smoke and Tam departs
Tam skelpit oan past the Skinflat Riggs
Like Usain Bolt oan syrup o' figs.

Whiles peukin in the driver's seat
Whiles haudin his heid tryin no tae greet
Whilst glowerin roond tae hae a keek
For polis playin hide and seek.

By this time Tam wis seein' double
Come whit may he'd be in trouble
He passed Bothkennar. Then the dyes
His trooser's wringin', he had wet thighs.

Tam McAirthur

The Leith Poleith he tried to say
Frae side to side the car did sway
When a' at once Tam saw a sign
Bo'ness two miles... or wis it nine
He'd loast his wey in his drunken haze
And swung the wheel in a dreamy daze
As Tam went roond the roundabout
And passed his turn he bellowed oot
Fegs and blast! I've gawn right past
He began reversin... awfi fast.

And scarcely had he backwards started
When bang! The car and bumper parted.
Tam stumbled tae the car behind
And was astonished there tae find
The driver no unlike oor man
Had been havin a swig at the Babycham
Through part drunk and partly anger
And seein the state o' his auld banger
The ither driver raved and ranted
Tae phone the polis aff he panted.
Noo Tam oh Tam, You'll get whits coamin
Yer breath is absolutely hummin!

Tam McAirthur

And as he thus bemoaned his fate
He hudnae very long tae wait
Before the polis, blue light flashin
Arrived in customary fashion.
A tap upon the window pane
There stood the polis in the rain.

Evening sir, said a friendly tone
You'd better get hame, leave well alone
That drunken eedjit in behind
Will insist oan swearin blind
That you reversed intae his car
Oan a roundabout... "Whit a star!"

Noo wha this tale o' truth shall read
Ilk man and mither's son tak heed
Whene'er tae drink ye are inclined
And drivin hame runs in yer mind
Think! Ye'd better nae be oe'r plucky
Tam McAirthur wis awfie lucky.

The Prisoner

Here I am a prisoner
Although without a cell
I'm deprived of life's enjoyments
My life? A living hell
Outside... eyes they follow me
Fingers pointing in my wake
Snatches of conversations say
OH NO! For goodness sake
They look at me with pity
But deep inside I cry
As their whispered conversations
Say I deserve to die.

I walk into a café
Someone offers me a chair
But the disdainful looks from management
Say I won't get served in there.

The Prisoner

I look at them
They look away
Faces pointed to the sky
And their whispered conversations
Say, I deserve to die.

What is this affliction
That makes life lasting torment
What is this affliction
When friends treat you with contempt
What is this affliction
That's condemned us once gay blades
Some say it's a virus
Others call it AIDS.

It's not long now I hear them say
Till death gives me release
From their whispered conversations
At last I'll be at peace.

Love Lost (1)

Last night as I lay on a pillow of bog myrtle
I dreamt we lay side by side
Staring at the milky way
And as we gazed
We drew lines in the sky with our fingers
Joining up the stars in a love knot of shared emotions

When I awoke I woke alone.

Alone remembering strolls in Callendar Wood
With the loch reflecting the moonlight's dancing
Alone as our laughter on the silver sands
Skipped over the Forth to Dun Eidan.

The perfect moments were always there
But my hammer tongue
Could never say, "I love you!"

Love Lost (2)

Sitting, looking at an empty chair
Wishing and hoping you were there
Silently offering up a prayer
To hold you near.

In my constellation you were the brightest star
For years I worshipped you, near and far
Then the heartache starts
In pain I screetch
As I remember you drifting out of reach.

Your cries for help? Only I could hear
Your face showed, twice. Then disappeared
Your cries still echo in my head
The waters rising with each tear I shed.

Now, sitting looking at an empty chair
Still wishing and hoping you were there
Silently offering up a prayer to hold you near
Facing the future, alone... I dread and fear.

FAWKIRK! (Mauchline's Shoap)

If I wis in Fawkirk High Street
I'd be in Mauchline's Shoap
Lookin for the stairs that Rabbie climbed
And the windae he screived oan
Wae his diamond pen
And I'd sweep the flair lookin for inspiration.

And if I was in Hope Street
I widnae be in the Coort Hoose
lookin for Correction
Nor in the Chapel lookin for Absolution
I'd be breengin doon tae Brockville Park
Lookin for a gemme.

And If I was in The Newmarket Bar
I wadnae be lookin for Tennent's Lager
Or a Fowlers Wee Happy Day
I'd be there lookin for my gaffer
As he planted his Elba oan the bar
And my wages in the till.

And when I was in Callendar Park
I'd be there in the gloaming
Wae Jeanie Mauchline
Lookin for the day
I could show her tae my Maw.

The First War Remembered (1)

A Foreign Field

In a corner of a foreign field
The poppy's blow,
But who brought the seed
Back here to grow.
Each bloom holds a memory
Painful for most.
While the banners in the churches
Hold a Regimental boast.

The First War Remembered (2)

The Soldiers Return

When we marched away
The weeping willow hung in green.
Now I return through, mist and rain
Hungry and thirsty.
Weeping in my heart, for a Home
And a Country
No longer fit for purpose.

The Purple Years

We never met in the full flush of youth
With desire giving way to passion
In our purple years
There can be no jealousy of what went before

So come to me
On another man's shoulders
Come to me
With fifty men in your hair
Come to me
In widowhood with one hundred men laid at your feet
Come to me
As the River Ganges with a thousand men
Drowning in your smile

Come to me and bring them all
In our world there's only time for fun.

Gold Digger

When the fire in your eye
Fades as you look at me,
It will be time to cut the roots
That anchor me to your shore

But if the drumbeat in your heart
Beats stronger as I near,
In sickness and in health
I will share your wealth.

Swing For Her

Swing child swing, Catch the sky.
Make the playground ring
With laughter.

Go on my son,
Push the swing higher
Your mother's watching, TERRIFIER!

Sailing From Shawbost (Isle of Lewis)

The whispering sails are calling me
I did not come to the edge of the world
The edge of Humanity
To listen to a dead language.
But when I look out, I hear the Salt White
Sails of Minerva calling,
Calling on me to join the crew.
I did not come to listen to a dead language,
But I am here, ready for the call.

I hear the moans of the women
From deep within the black house.
And they too are waiting. Waiting for the sea
Giving back their men, their dead men.
And in the black house,
They weave an unholy joy into their moaning
Whilst waiting their promotion to widowhood.
And their promotion will come,
The call will come... In years to come.

MacCaig's Toad R.I.P.

Frogs sit more solid than toads
Move much neater than toads
But still get squashed on roads
The same as toads.

What pioneering spirit drives the frog and toad
To see what lies across the road
It takes four leaps or five or ten
Alright in darkness, but when
The headlights flash, there's a frog in my throat
Thrown up by the wheels of a turboed milk float.

I wish that frogs could be like men
And use bridges and tunnels, again and again
And stop the carnage on our roads
And the pavement memorials to frogs and toads.

The Wellman Clinic

I went tae the boozer
Tae meet my best mate
And efter a couple o' goldies
We were baith feelin great

Wae a good bit o' craic
It was time tae go hame
So oot we baith stepped
In the stairroddin rain

Bit the rain's no a bad thing
When ye toddle oot the boozers
Coz that wey folks dinnae see
The pee stains doon yer troozers.

But wae complaints fae the missus
I had tae gie in
She's had mair thrills fae her Hotpoint
Than she ever got fae mine.

The Wellman Clinic

So I went tae the doctor
The good doctor Mike
And said "When I was younger
I could pee right ower the dyke."

But wae talkin tae you
I've got nothing tae lose
As the dreeps fae my wee man
Takes the shine aff my shoes.

And when I go tae the loo
My heids a' a flutter
When I haundle it right
It flows right doon the gutter.

But if my touch it desserts me
As sometimes before
A ring o' bright watter
Is seen oan the floor.

The Wellman Clinic

So tell me dear Doctor
What should I know
What should I do
When I'm needin tae go?
Well he poked and he pawed
He hummed and he hawed
Then said... These symptoms
They're not new. You see
The answers quite simple
There's not even a fee,
When you go to the toilet
Sit doon tae pee.

Fawkirk & Burns

(1)

The skill weans were scunnert.
There in thir open books wiz a new poem
Nailed ti the page.
"Tae a mouse!" "ti be learned bi hert"
Said the Dominie.

Words like thristles and thorns
Ploughed through thir winter language
This wey and that till they funt shelter
In a few young wunderin minds.

Years later, wi a skirl o' the pipes
And a flash o' tartan
A harvest of words wiz reaped
Fae a bog road council hoose.

(2)

The Auld men said the name Rabbie Burns
As if he fermed jist yesterday at
Carmuirs, Bothkenner, or Kinneil.

Fawkirk & Burns

Whit a man!, Whit a man
They'd say, shakin their heids smiling.
Aye, whit a man for the Uisge
Whit a man for the weemin.

It wiz important ti the auld codgers
That Rabbie wiz a puir man
Like thirsel's a toil bent fermer.

(3)
Jist aff the High Street,
Doon a cawsie close,
Wafted a torrent o' January sounds.
Bonny Jean. Mary Morrison. Ae Fond Kiss.

A young fermer tried his luck
Across the Wheatsheaf Bar.
"Is Burns still alive?"
His speirin wis met wae mockery and mirth.

There wiz aye time for a barleycorn pause
Atween a quote, a stave o' sang,
And the chuckin oot
O' some smertie takin the Mick.

The Tutor

A mis-related participle
Is never ever admissible
You know it throws the reader
Right off track.

And the danger of bad spelling
In a story you are telling
Can persuade the truth to lie,
A known fact.

But the part that is most galling
When writing is your calling
Is suffering your tutor's
Lack of tact.

Falkirk Writers Circle

Visit us
The Circle meet every Tuesday evening in the
Greenpark Community Centre, Polmont, at
7.30pm. New members are made welcome and
given encouragement and assistance.

Contact
Chairman: Gordon Brown
Email: gophb81@gmail.com
Secretary: Isobel Quinn
Email: isobel.quinn@outlook.com

writers'
umbrella

Writers Umbrella

SUBMISSIONS & QUERIES: editor.
writersumbrella@gmail.com

Jen Butler,
16 Norval Place,
Rosyth
KY11 2RJ

Membership of FDACC is open to groups who are engaged in activities which add to the artistic life of Falkirk or whose aims and activities encourage an awareness in civic amenity.

Groups seeking membership should contact Secretary jamieorourke@live.co.uk enclosing a copy of their constitution, or a statement of the aims and objectives of their group, along with a list of current office bearers.